PRINCEWILL LAGANG

From Side Hustle to Main Hustle: Making Your Passion Profitable

Contents

1

The Journey Begins

In the world of dreams and ambitions, there exists a realm where the lines between work and passion blur, and where the pursuit of profit is fueled by the fires of personal fulfillment. This is the world of side hustles, those endeavors that start as small, personal passions but have the potential to evolve into your main hustle, your primary source of income. In this book, we embark on a journey through the exciting, challenging, and often rewarding landscape of transforming your side hustle into your main hustle.

The Side Hustle: A Ray of Hope

Imagine this: it's a quiet evening, and you're hunched over a workbench in your garage, meticulously crafting a piece of furniture. Or perhaps you're in your cozy kitchen, perfecting the secret recipe for the salsa that your friends and family can't get enough of. These moments represent your side hustle, a labor of love that you engage in outside your regular job, an expression of your passion and creativity.

Side hustles are born from a combination of our talents, interests, and the simple desire to create something meaningful. They are a ray of hope that offers us a taste of freedom, autonomy, and financial independence. But they can also be demanding, challenging, and uncertain. That's why, for many of us, side hustles remain just that - a side project, a fleeting hobby. But what if your side hustle could be more than that? What if you could turn your passion into your livelihood, and make your side hustle your main hustle?

Why Transform Your Side Hustle?

The answer is simple: because it's possible, and because you deserve to do work that fulfills you. Turning your side hustle into your main hustle isn't a pipe dream; it's a tangible goal that countless individuals have achieved.

1. Freedom and Autonomy: When your side hustle becomes your main hustle, you gain control over your time and your financial destiny. You decide when and where you work, and your success depends on your choices and efforts.

2. Passion Meets Profit: Few things are more rewarding than doing what you love and getting paid for it. Turning your passion into a profitable endeavor isn't just a financial win; it's a personal victory that can lead to a more fulfilling life.

3. A Chance to Grow: Your side hustle might be a small operation right now, but with the right strategy, it has the potential to grow into a full-fledged business. This growth provides a sense of achievement and opens up opportunities you never thought possible.

4. Financial Security: In an ever-changing job market, having a successful side hustle can be a safety net. It can be your Plan B or even your Plan A, ensuring that you're not solely dependent on a single source of income.

What This Book Offers

In the pages that follow, we will explore the path from side hustle to main hustle, covering everything from setting goals and refining your idea to marketing, scaling, and overcoming challenges. Each chapter is designed to equip you with the knowledge, tools, and inspiration needed to navigate this journey successfully.

Whether you're crafting handmade jewelry, writing a blog, developing software, or cooking up a storm in your kitchen, this book is for you. It doesn't matter if your side hustle is a hobby, a creative endeavor, or a service you offer – the principles and strategies we discuss are applicable to a wide range of endeavors.

Remember, this journey won't be without its challenges, but that's what makes it worth it. So, let's embark on this exciting journey together, from side hustle to main hustle. It's time to make your passion profitable.

In the chapters that follow, we'll delve into the process of identifying, developing, and scaling your side hustle, and you'll learn how to navigate the often daunting terrain of entrepreneurship. We'll explore the nuts and bolts of turning your passion into profit, with practical advice, real-life examples, and actionable steps to help you achieve your dream.

So, fasten your seatbelt, gather your passion, and let's get started on the adventure of a lifetime – making your side hustle your main hustle!

2

Defining Your Side Hustle

Your journey from a side hustle to a main hustle begins with a clear understanding of what your side hustle is and what it can become. This chapter is all about defining and refining your side hustle, helping you lay a solid foundation for the transformation ahead.

The Seed of Your Passion

Imagine a tree, with its roots deep in the ground, its trunk strong and stable, and its branches reaching for the sky. Your side hustle is like a seed, the potential for that tree, and in this chapter, we're going to plant it firmly in the ground.

1. What's Your Passion?

The first step is to identify what you're truly passionate about. Think about the activities that light you up, the projects that you eagerly dive into, and the hobbies that make you lose track of time. Your side hustle should align with these passions. Whether it's crafting, writing, coding, cooking, or any other pursuit, the foundation of your side hustle must be something you genuinely love.

2. Clarify Your Purpose

Next, consider why you're pursuing this side hustle. Is it to make a living doing something you love, to share your talent with the world, to have more control over your time, or for some other reason? Your purpose is your guiding star, so be clear about it from the start.

The Idea Behind the Side Hustle

Now that you've identified your passion and purpose, it's time to refine your side hustle idea. Your side hustle must offer value to others, and it should ideally solve a problem or fulfill a need.

3. Who Is Your Audience?

Define your target audience or customer base. Who are the people most likely to be interested in what you're offering? Understanding your audience is essential for tailoring your side hustle to their needs.

4. Unique Selling Proposition (USP)

What sets your side hustle apart from the competition? What makes it unique? Your Unique Selling Proposition (USP) is your secret sauce. It could be the quality of your handmade products, your expertise in a niche, your one-of-a-kind approach, or your exceptional customer service.

5. Market Research

Take the time to research the market. What are similar businesses or individuals doing? What are the trends and opportunities in your chosen field? Market research will help you understand the competitive landscape and make informed decisions.

The Viability Test

Before fully committing to your side hustle, you need to assess its viability. While passion and purpose are crucial, the business side of things can't be ignored.

6. Financial Feasibility

Calculate the potential costs and revenues of your side hustle. How much will it cost to get started, and how much can you realistically earn? Create a basic financial plan to ensure your side hustle is financially viable.

7. Time Commitment

Evaluate how much time you can realistically dedicate to your side hustle. Consider your current job, family commitments, and other responsibilities. Your side hustle should fit into your schedule without overwhelming you.

8. Resources and Skills

Identify the resources and skills you have and those you might need to develop. Do you have the necessary tools, equipment, or knowledge to start? Are there areas where you need to upskill?

The Elevator Pitch

In just a few sentences, can you explain what your side hustle is, why it's valuable, and who it's for? Crafting a compelling elevator pitch is a valuable exercise that helps you articulate the essence of your side hustle.

9. Crafting Your Elevator Pitch

Practice describing your side hustle in a concise and engaging manner. It should be clear, memorable, and leave a strong impression on anyone you share it with.

The Next Steps

Once you've defined your side hustle, passion, and purpose, and assessed its viability, you're ready to move forward. The next chapter will guide you through the process of setting goals and creating a roadmap for your side hustle journey.

Remember, your side hustle is not set in stone. It's a dynamic entity that can evolve over time. By defining it clearly from the outset, you'll have a strong foundation to build upon as you transform your side hustle into your main hustle.

In the chapters that follow, we'll delve deeper into the practical steps you can take to refine and grow your side hustle. We'll explore goal setting, planning, and action-taking, helping you turn your passion into profit one step at a time.

3

Setting Goals and Creating Your Roadmap

Now that you've defined your side hustle, it's time to set clear goals and create a roadmap for your journey from side hustle to main hustle. In this chapter, we'll explore the importance of goal setting, how to establish SMART goals, and how to design a roadmap to guide your efforts.

The Power of Setting Goals

Goals provide a sense of direction, purpose, and motivation. When it comes to turning your side hustle into your main hustle, having well-defined goals is crucial.

1. Why Goals Matter
   - Goals give you a clear target to aim for.
   - They help you measure progress.
   - They keep you motivated during challenges.
   - They guide your decision-making.

SMART Goals: A Blueprint for Success

To ensure your goals are effective, they should be SMART:

2. Specific

Your goals should be clear and specific. Avoid vague or broad objectives. For example, "I want to increase my side hustle income" is not specific enough. Instead, aim for something like, "I want to double my side hustle income within the next year."

3. Measurable

Your goals should be quantifiable. You should be able to track your progress and know when you've achieved them. Using the previous example, you can measure your income to determine whether you've doubled it or not.

4. Achievable

While you want your goals to be ambitious, they should also be realistic. Consider your current resources, time, and skills. Setting unattainable goals can lead to frustration and disappointment.

5. Relevant

Your goals should align with your passion and purpose. They should be relevant to what you want to achieve with your side hustle. Ensure that they make sense in the context of your business.

6. Time-Bound

Set a timeframe for your goals. When do you want to achieve them? Having a deadline adds a sense of urgency and helps you prioritize your tasks.

Creating Your Roadmap

With SMART goals in place, it's time to create a roadmap that outlines the steps you need to take to achieve those goals.

7. Break Down Your Goals

Divide your SMART goals into smaller, manageable tasks or milestones. These smaller steps make the path to your main hustle less overwhelming.

8. Prioritize Tasks

Determine which tasks are most critical to achieving your goals and prioritize them. This will help you focus your time and energy on the most important actions.

9. Develop a Timeline

Create a timeline that includes deadlines for each task or milestone. A clear schedule helps you stay on track and ensures that you're making consistent progress.

10. Allocate Resources

Identify the resources you'll need to accomplish your goals. This could include time, money, tools, or assistance from others. Ensure you have what you need to move forward.

Review and Adapt

Your roadmap is not set in stone. As you progress, you may encounter unexpected challenges, opportunities, or changes in your circumstances. Regularly review and adapt your goals and roadmap as needed.

11. Regular Evaluation

Periodically assess your progress. Are you on track to achieve your goals? If not, what adjustments are necessary?

12. Be Open to Change

Flexibility is key. Embrace change when it makes sense. Your goals and roadmap should evolve as your side hustle grows.

Next Steps

With your goals set and your roadmap in place, you're well-prepared to navigate the journey from side hustle to main hustle. In the chapters that follow, we'll delve into specific strategies and tactics to help you achieve your goals and make your passion profitable.

Remember, the key to success lies not just in setting goals but in taking consistent action to reach them. So, stay motivated, be persistent, and keep your eyes on the prize as you transform your side hustle into your main hustle.

4

Branding Your Side Hustle

In the journey from side hustle to main hustle, effective branding plays a pivotal role. Your brand is how you present your side hustle to the world, and it's what sets you apart from the competition. In this chapter, we'll explore the importance of branding and how to build a strong brand for your side hustle.

The Power of Branding

Branding goes far beyond just having a catchy logo or a well-designed website. It's about creating a consistent and compelling identity that resonates with your audience. Here's why branding matters:

1. Establishes Trust

A strong brand inspires trust and credibility. When potential customers see a professional and consistent brand, they're more likely to engage with your side hustle.

2. Differentiates You

Your brand distinguishes you from your competitors. It communicates what makes your side hustle unique and why customers should choose you.

3. Creates Recognition

Consistent branding makes you easily recognizable. It helps people remember your side hustle and builds a sense of familiarity.

4. Builds Loyalty

A strong brand can create customer loyalty. People are more likely to return to a brand they trust and have a positive experience with.

Defining Your Brand

Before you can build a brand, you need to understand what your brand represents. This involves defining your brand's personality, values, and mission.

5. Brand Personality

Think of your brand as a person. What personality traits would best describe it? Is your brand serious and professional, playful and creative, or somewhere in between?

6. Brand Values

What values does your brand stand for? Consider the principles and beliefs that guide your business. For example, environmental sustainability, quality, or innovation.

7. Brand Mission

Your brand's mission is its purpose, beyond making a profit. What are you trying to achieve or change in the world? Your mission should align with your passion and purpose.

Visual Identity

The visual elements of your brand are what people see and remember. Your visual identity includes your logo, color scheme, typography, and overall design.

8. Logo

Your logo is the face of your brand. It should be simple, memorable, and reflective of your brand's personality. Consider hiring a professional designer if you're not skilled in graphic design.

9. Color Scheme

Colors evoke emotions and can convey the essence of your brand. Choose colors that align with your brand's personality and values.

10. Typography

Select fonts that match your brand's personality and ensure readability in your marketing materials.

Consistency is Key

Consistency is vital in branding. Every interaction your audience has with your brand should reinforce your brand identity.

11. Brand Guidelines

Create brand guidelines that outline how your brand elements should be used. This includes details about the logo's placement, color codes, and fonts.

12. Online and Offline Presence

Maintain consistency in your online presence (website, social media) and offline presence (business cards, packaging). Ensure that your brand looks and feels the same across all platforms.

Brand Storytelling

A compelling brand story can connect with your audience on a deeper level. It's the narrative that explains your brand's origins, mission, and values.

13. Craft Your Story

Write a compelling story that relates your journey, what drives your passion, and the impact you want to make. Share this story on your website and in marketing materials.

14. Share Authentic Content

Be authentic in your storytelling. Share your challenges, successes, and the people behind your side hustle. Authenticity builds trust and connections.

Next Steps

As you continue on your journey from side hustle to main hustle, remember that branding is an ongoing process. Your brand may evolve over time, just as your side hustle grows. In the chapters that follow, we'll explore marketing strategies and tactics to help you promote your brand and attract a loyal customer base.

By building a strong and memorable brand, you'll be well-prepared to make your passion profitable and stand out in your chosen market.

5

Marketing Your Side Hustle

In the journey from side hustle to main hustle, marketing is your bridge to reaching a wider audience and growing your business. This chapter explores various marketing strategies and tactics to help you effectively promote your side hustle and connect with potential customers.

The Role of Marketing

Marketing is about more than just selling; it's about creating relationships with your audience. Effective marketing can help you achieve the following:

1. Attract New Customers

Reach and engage with people who may not have known about your side hustle.

2. Retain Existing Customers

Nurture relationships with current customers, encouraging repeat business and loyalty.

3. Build Brand Awareness

Increase recognition of your brand and what it represents.

4. Drive Sales and Revenue

Convince potential customers to purchase your products or services.

Understanding Your Target Audience

Before diving into marketing strategies, it's crucial to understand your target audience. Knowing who your ideal customers are helps you tailor your marketing efforts.

2. Create Buyer Personas

Develop detailed buyer personas that include demographic information, interests, challenges, and goals. These personas guide your marketing decisions.

3. Identify Pain Points

Understand the problems or pain points your target audience faces that your side hustle can solve.

4. Determine Where They Hang Out

Know where your audience spends their time, both online and offline. This helps you choose the right marketing channels.

Online Marketing

The digital world offers numerous opportunities for marketing your side hustle. Here are some key online marketing strategies:

5. Website

Create a professional website that showcases your products or services, your brand story, and a way for customers to contact or purchase from you.

6. Content Marketing

Write blog posts, create videos, or produce other valuable content related to your niche. Share this content on your website and through social media to establish your expertise.

7. Social Media Marketing

Choose social media platforms that align with your target audience's preferences. Regularly share content, engage with your audience, and use paid advertising if it makes sense for your business.

8. Email Marketing

Build an email list of interested prospects and customers. Send newsletters, promotions, and updates to keep them engaged.

Offline Marketing

Don't forget about offline marketing, which can be especially effective for certain types of side hustles:

9. Networking

Attend industry events, local gatherings, and meetups to connect with potential customers and other professionals.

10. Local Advertising

Use traditional advertising methods such as flyers, posters, and local newspapers to reach a local audience.

11. Direct Mail

Send postcards or letters to potential customers in your target area.

Paid Advertising

Paid advertising can help you reach a broader audience quickly:

12. Google Ads

Use Google Ads to appear at the top of search results when people are looking for products or services like yours.

13. Social Media Ads

Create targeted ad campaigns on social media platforms to reach specific demographics.

Analytics and Metrics

To assess the effectiveness of your marketing efforts, it's essential to track key metrics:

14. Website Analytics

Use tools like Google Analytics to monitor website traffic, user behavior, and conversion rates.

15. Social Media Insights

Analyze data from your social media accounts to understand which posts and campaigns are most successful.

16. Email Campaign Metrics

Track open rates, click-through rates, and conversion rates for your email campaigns.

Marketing Plan

Develop a comprehensive marketing plan that outlines your strategies, goals, and a schedule for executing your marketing efforts. Your plan should be adaptable and regularly reviewed.

Next Steps

In the chapters that follow, we'll dive deeper into specific marketing strategies and tactics, helping you create a marketing plan tailored to your side hustle. By effectively marketing your side hustle, you'll reach new customers and continue to grow your business on your journey from side hustle to main hustle.

Remember that marketing is an ongoing process, and success may require some trial and error. Stay committed, adapt to changes in your industry and audience, and continue to refine your marketing efforts to connect with your ideal customers.

6

Sales and Customer Relationships

Now that you've defined your brand and developed your marketing strategy, the next crucial step in your journey from side hustle to main hustle is to focus on sales and building strong customer relationships. This chapter delves into effective sales techniques and strategies for fostering loyal customers.

The Art of Selling

Sales are at the heart of every successful business. Whether you're selling products, services, or both, mastering the art of selling is essential.

1. Understand the Needs of Your Customers

To make a sale, you must first understand the needs, desires, and challenges of your customers. What problems can your side hustle solve for them?

2. Effective Communication

Learn to communicate your value clearly. Be a good listener, ask open-ended questions, and provide tailored solutions to your customers.

3. Overcome Objections

Expect objections from potential customers and have responses ready. Address concerns, offer alternatives, and highlight the benefits of your offerings.

4. Close the Sale

When the time is right, confidently ask for the sale. Use closing techniques that are appropriate for your business, such as trial closes, summarization, or limited-time offers.

Building Strong Customer Relationships

Successful businesses don't just focus on making one-time sales; they aim to build long-term customer relationships.

5. Exceptional Customer Service

Provide outstanding customer service at every touchpoint. Respond promptly to inquiries, resolve issues, and make the customer feel valued.

6. Personalization

Tailor your interactions to each customer. Remember their preferences, celebrate their milestones, and show that you care about their individual needs.

7. Loyalty Programs

Create loyalty programs that reward repeat customers. Offer discounts, exclusive access, or personalized offers to encourage loyalty.

8. Feedback and Improvement

Encourage customer feedback and actively use it to improve your products or services. Show customers that their opinions matter.

Upselling and Cross-Selling

Increasing the value of each transaction is a smart way to boost your revenue. Consider these strategies:

9. Upselling
   Encourage customers to purchase a more expensive version of your product or add premium features. For example, offer a larger-sized product with a discount.

10. Cross-Selling
   Suggest complementary products or services that enhance what the customer is already buying. For example, if you sell laptops, offer accessories like cases or wireless mice.

Managing Customer Feedback

Feedback can be an invaluable tool for growth:

11. Online Reviews
   Encourage customers to leave reviews on platforms like Google, Yelp, or your website. Respond to both positive and negative reviews professionally.

12. Surveys and Questionnaires
   Send out surveys or questionnaires to gather insights on customer experiences and areas for improvement.

13. Social Media Listening
   Monitor social media channels for mentions of your brand. Address any issues or feedback promptly.

Handling Dissatisfied Customers

Not every customer will be satisfied, and how you handle these situations can make a difference:

14. Apologize and Resolve

If a customer is dissatisfied, apologize for their experience and take steps to make it right.

15. Learn from Feedback

Use negative feedback as an opportunity to improve your products, services, and customer experience.

Next Steps

As you continue on your journey from side hustle to main hustle, remember that sales and customer relationships are central to your success. Your satisfied customers can become your most effective marketing tool through word-of-mouth referrals.

In the chapters that follow, we'll explore scaling your side hustle and tackling the challenges that come with growth. By mastering the art of selling and fostering strong customer relationships, you're well-prepared to take your side hustle to the next level.

Remember that the quality of your customer relationships will contribute significantly to your side hustle's growth and profitability. Treat each customer interaction as an opportunity to build trust, loyalty, and a positive reputation for your business.

7

Scaling Your Side Hustle

With a strong foundation in branding, marketing, sales, and customer relationships, you're now ready to take your side hustle to the next level. In this chapter, we'll explore the strategies and tactics for scaling your side hustle and expanding your business.

The Need for Scaling

Scaling your side hustle is about growing your business in a sustainable and profitable way. While it might be tempting to expand quickly, it's crucial to do so thoughtfully to ensure long-term success.

1. Why Scale?
   - To reach a larger audience and serve more customers.
   - To increase revenue and profitability.
   - To create efficiencies and streamline operations.
   - To realize your vision of making your side hustle your main hustle.

Diversify Your Offerings

One of the ways to scale is by diversifying your products or services:

2. Product Line Expansion

Develop new products that align with your brand and cater to your existing customer base or target audience.

3. Service Expansion

If you offer services, consider offering additional services or packages to provide more value to your customers.

4. Bundling and Upselling

Create bundles or packages of your existing products or services to encourage customers to purchase more.

Automate and Streamline

Efficiency is key to scaling. Consider automating and streamlining your operations:

5. Use Technology

Invest in tools and software that can automate tasks like customer management, inventory tracking, and marketing.

6. Outsourcing

Consider outsourcing tasks such as customer support, fulfillment, or marketing to experts in those areas.

7. Streamline Processes

Continuously evaluate your business processes and look for ways to make them more efficient and cost-effective.

Expand Your Market

To scale, you may need to expand your target market or reach a broader audience:

8. New Geographical Markets

Explore selling your products or services in new geographic regions or even internationally.

9. Online Marketplaces

Consider selling on online marketplaces like Amazon or Etsy to reach a wider customer base.

10. Partnerships

Form strategic partnerships with other businesses to tap into their customer networks.

Funding and Capital

Scaling often requires financial resources. Consider your options for funding:

11. Bootstrapping

Use your side hustle's profits to fund its growth gradually.

12. Loans and Grants

Explore small business loans, grants, or crowdfunding to secure additional capital.

13. Investors and Equity Financing

Consider seeking investors or offering equity in your business in exchange for capital.

Monitor and Adjust

Scaling is an ongoing process. Regularly monitor your progress and adjust your strategy as needed:

14. Key Performance Indicators (KPIs)

Identify and track KPIs that are relevant to your business to gauge performance.

15. Feedback Loops

Create feedback loops with customers, employees, and partners to stay informed about areas that need improvement.

16. Be Adaptable

Be ready to pivot your strategy if market conditions or other factors change.

Next Steps

Scaling your side hustle is a significant step on your journey from a side hustle to your main hustle. While it's an exciting phase, it also comes with challenges. In the chapters that follow, we'll explore how to tackle these challenges, manage growth, and maintain the quality and values that define your brand.

Remember, scaling should be aligned with your vision and purpose. Don't lose sight of why you started your side hustle in the first place. With the right strategies and a commitment to maintaining your brand's integrity, you can successfully scale your side hustle and turn it into your main hustle.

8

Challenges and Solutions

As you work to transform your side hustle into your main hustle, you're likely to encounter various challenges along the way. This chapter will help you anticipate, understand, and address these challenges effectively.

Common Challenges

Starting and growing a business is no small feat. Here are some common challenges you may face:

1. Financial Challenges
    - Insufficient capital to cover expenses.
    - Cash flow issues, especially in the early stages.
    - Balancing personal finances with business expenses.

2. Time Management
    - Juggling your side hustle with other responsibilities.
    - Finding time for business development and growth.
    - Avoiding burnout and maintaining work-life balance.

3. Marketing and Sales
   - Attracting and retaining customers.
   - Navigating marketing strategies effectively.
   - Scaling sales and building a customer base.

4. Competition and Market Changes
   - Staying ahead in a competitive market.
   - Adapting to industry changes and trends.
   - Responding to new competitors.

5. Scaling and Managing Growth
   - Balancing growth with quality.
   - Managing increased demand and operational challenges.
   - Scaling without sacrificing the essence of your brand.

Problem-Solving Strategies

When facing these challenges, consider these strategies to overcome them:

6. Financial Management
   - Develop a detailed financial plan.
   - Build a financial cushion for unexpected expenses.
   - Seek advice from financial professionals.

7. Time Management
   - Prioritize tasks and focus on high-impact activities.
   - Delegate or outsource tasks that can be handled by others.
   - Establish a well-structured schedule.

8. Marketing and Sales
   - Continuously assess and adjust your marketing strategies.
   - Invest in training or outsourcing if necessary.
   - Cultivate strong customer relationships and prioritize repeat business.

9. Adaptation and Innovation
   - Stay informed about industry trends and market changes.
   - Innovate and adapt your offerings as needed.
   - Consider partnerships or collaborations to stay competitive.

10. Growth Management
   - Maintain a customer-centric approach as you scale.
   - Implement effective systems and processes to handle growth.
   - Seek guidance from mentors or advisors with experience in business expansion.

Resilience and Mindset

Dealing with challenges requires resilience and a positive mindset:

11. Embrace Failure as a Learning Opportunity
   Accept that setbacks and failures are part of the journey. Learn from them and use them to grow.

12. Stay Committed to Your Vision
   Remind yourself of your passion, purpose, and the reasons you started your side hustle. This can help you stay motivated during difficult times.

13. Seek Support
   Don't hesitate to seek support and advice from mentors, peers, or business networks. Sometimes, sharing your challenges with others can lead to valuable insights.

Conclusion

Transforming your side hustle into your main hustle is a rewarding journey, but it's not without its challenges. The key to success is to anticipate these challenges, develop strategies to address them, and maintain a resilient mindset throughout the process.

In the chapters that follow, we'll delve into maintaining the quality and values that define your brand as you navigate growth and success. By understanding and effectively addressing challenges, you'll be better prepared to reach your goals and make your passion profitable.

Remember, the challenges you face are opportunities for growth and improvement. Each obstacle you overcome brings you one step closer to realizing your dream of turning your side hustle into your main hustle.

9

Preserving Your Brand Values

As your side hustle evolves into your main hustle, it's essential to maintain the core values and essence that define your brand. This chapter explores how to preserve your brand values and ensure that your business continues to reflect your passion and purpose.

The Importance of Brand Values

Your brand values are the principles, beliefs, and standards that define your business. They shape your brand identity and influence the way you operate. Preserving these values is crucial for maintaining the authenticity and reputation of your brand.

1. Consistency and Trust

Consistency in upholding your brand values builds trust with your customers. When they know what to expect, they are more likely to remain loyal.

2. Brand Differentiation

Your brand values distinguish you from competitors. They are what make your brand unique and attract like-minded customers.

3. Business Ethics

Upholding your values ensures ethical business practices, which can have a positive impact on your reputation and relationships with customers and stakeholders.

Identifying Your Brand Values

Before you can preserve your brand values, you need to clearly define them. Ask yourself:

4. What Do You Stand For?

Consider the core principles and beliefs that guide your business. Is it quality, sustainability, innovation, community involvement, or something else?

5. What Sets You Apart?

Identify what makes your brand unique and how your values distinguish you from competitors.

6. What Drives Your Passion?

Reflect on the personal motivations and passions that led you to start your side hustle. These are often closely tied to your brand values.

Integrating Values into Your Business

Once you've identified your brand values, it's important to integrate them into your business operations and culture.

7. Align with Your Team

Ensure that your team members, if you have any, understand and embrace your brand values. This alignment fosters a consistent and cohesive brand culture.

8. Customer Interactions

Train your employees to reflect your values in customer interactions. Your values should be evident in the customer experience.

9. Marketing and Messaging

Craft marketing messages and content that align with your brand values. This helps reinforce your values in the minds of your audience.

Staying True During Growth

Preserving your brand values can be challenging, especially as your business grows. Here's how to maintain your values:

10. Set Boundaries

Clearly define what you won't compromise on, even as your business expands. These non-negotiable values act as anchors for your brand.

11. Regular Evaluation

Periodically review your brand values and make adjustments if needed. Values can evolve as your business grows and changes.

12. Lead by Example

As the leader of your business, exemplify your values in your actions and decisions. Your team and customers will look to you for guidance.

Communication and Transparency

Effective communication is key to preserving your brand values:

13. Transparent Business Practices

Be transparent about your business practices and values. Share your commitment to these values with your customers and the public.

14. Addressing Challenges
When faced with challenges or decisions that might test your values, address them openly with your team and customers. Transparency builds trust.

Next Steps

In the chapters that follow, we'll explore maintaining quality and consistent brand experiences as your business grows. By preserving your brand values and ensuring that they remain at the core of your business, you'll continue to attract customers who resonate with your mission and values.

Remember, your brand values are the guiding principles that shape your brand's identity and reputation. By staying true to these values, you'll not only maintain the essence of your brand but also strengthen the connections with your customers.

10

Maintaining Quality and Consistency

As your side hustle transitions into your main hustle, it becomes increasingly important to maintain the quality and consistency that your brand is known for. This chapter explores strategies and best practices for upholding the standards that have defined your brand and contributed to your success.

The Significance of Quality and Consistency

Quality and consistency are the cornerstones of a successful brand. They help build trust, loyalty, and a positive reputation among your customers and in the market.

1. Customer Trust

Consistently delivering high-quality products or services establishes trust with your customers. They know they can rely on your brand.

2. Brand Loyalty

Quality and consistency contribute to brand loyalty. Customers who have positive, consistent experiences are more likely to return and recommend your brand to others.

3. Positive Reputation

Maintaining quality and consistency helps build a positive reputation in your industry. This reputation can attract new customers and opportunities.

Upholding Quality

Quality starts with the products or services you provide. Here's how to ensure quality:

4. Set Standards

Establish clear quality standards for your offerings. This might involve detailed specifications, testing procedures, or quality control measures.

5. Regular Evaluation

Continuously assess the quality of your products or services. Monitor customer feedback and use it to make improvements.

6. Training and Development

Invest in training and development for your team to ensure they understand and can maintain your quality standards.

Maintaining Consistency

Consistency applies to all aspects of your business, from your branding to customer interactions. Here's how to maintain it:

7. Brand Guidelines

Create comprehensive brand guidelines that cover your visual identity, tone of voice, and customer experience.

8. Employee Training

Train your employees on your brand guidelines and the importance of consistency in customer interactions.

9. Customer Experience

Ensure a consistent customer experience across all touchpoints, from your website to in-person interactions.

Problem-Solving for Consistency

Maintaining consistency can be challenging, especially as your business grows. Here's how to address common consistency issues:

10. Scalability

Develop scalable processes that allow you to maintain consistency as your business expands. Automate tasks when possible.

11. Communication

Foster open communication with your team to address any inconsistencies promptly.

12. Feedback and Adaptation

Use feedback from customers and employees to identify areas where consistency may be lacking and make necessary adjustments.

Monitoring and Evaluation

To ensure quality and consistency, you need to monitor and evaluate your efforts:

13. Key Performance Indicators (KPIs)

Set KPIs related to quality and consistency, and track them regularly to ensure you meet your standards.

14. Regular Audits

Conduct periodic audits of your operations to identify any inconsistencies or quality issues.

15. Customer Feedback

Listen to customer feedback and take action to address any concerns related to quality or consistency.

Next Steps

In the chapters that follow, we'll explore maintaining your brand values and expanding your business further. By upholding quality and consistency, you not only maintain the trust and loyalty of your existing customers but also attract new ones who are looking for reliability and excellence.

Remember that quality and consistency are integral to the long-term success of your brand. Customers rely on your business to deliver as promised, and by doing so, you reinforce the positive reputation and trust that you've worked hard to build.

11

Expanding Your Horizons

With a solid foundation, maintained quality, and preserved brand values, it's time to look toward the horizon and explore opportunities for expanding your business. In this chapter, we'll delve into strategies for taking your side hustle to the next level and reaching new heights.

The Call of Expansion

Expanding your business is a natural progression in your journey from side hustle to main hustle. It allows you to reach more customers, increase revenue, and make a greater impact. Here's why expansion matters:

1. Growth and Revenue

Expansion can lead to increased sales, revenue, and profitability, helping you achieve your financial goals.

2. Market Opportunities

Expansion allows you to explore new markets, segments, and customer demographics.

3. Increased Impact

Expanding your business can help you make a more significant impact on your industry and community.

4. Competitive Advantage

By growing and evolving, you maintain a competitive edge in the market.

Diversify Your Offerings

Diversifying your products or services can be an effective way to expand your business:

5. New Product Lines

Develop new products that cater to your existing customer base or appeal to a broader audience.

6. Service Expansion

If you offer services, consider expanding your service offerings to provide more value to your customers.

7. Licensing and Franchising

Explore opportunities to license your brand or franchise your business to expand to new locations.

Geographic Expansion

Expanding to new geographic regions can open up new customer markets:

8. Local Expansion

If you're a local business, consider opening additional locations in neighboring areas.

9. National or International Markets

Explore the potential of expanding to national or international markets through e-commerce or distribution partnerships.

10. Online Marketplaces

List your products or services on online marketplaces like Amazon or eBay to reach a broader customer base.

Collaborations and Partnerships

Strategic partnerships can help you expand more efficiently:

11. Joint Ventures

Consider collaborating with complementary businesses to reach shared goals.

12. Distribution Partnerships

Partner with companies that can help you reach new audiences or markets more effectively.

Scaling Operations

To expand successfully, you need to scale your operations and capabilities:

13. Efficient Processes

Streamline your processes and workflows to accommodate increased demand.

14. Technology and Automation

Invest in technology and automation to handle higher volumes and increase efficiency.

15. Human Resources

Consider hiring additional staff or outsourcing tasks to support your growth.

Market Research and Analysis

Expanding into new markets requires thorough research:

16. Market Research

Conduct market research to understand the demand, competition, and customer preferences in your target market.

17. Feasibility Studies

Assess the feasibility of your expansion plans, including financial projections and potential risks.

18. Customer Feedback

Listen to feedback from your existing customers to identify areas where expansion could better serve their needs.

Next Steps

In the chapters that follow, we'll explore how to manage and adapt to the challenges that may arise during expansion. By strategically diversifying your offerings, expanding your reach, and forming partnerships, you'll be well-prepared to take your side hustle to new heights.

Remember that expansion is a dynamic process, and it's essential to stay true to your brand values and the quality that defines your business. By doing so, you'll continue to attract and retain customers as you grow.

12

Navigating Challenges in Expansion

As you expand your side hustle, you're likely to encounter various challenges and obstacles along the way. This chapter is dedicated to helping you navigate these challenges effectively, ensuring that your journey from side hustle to main hustle remains on course.

Common Challenges in Expansion

Expanding your business is an exciting but complex process, and it comes with its share of challenges:

1. Financial Challenges
   - Securing funding for expansion.
   - Managing increased operating costs.
   - Navigating cash flow challenges during growth.

2. Scalability
   - Adapting processes and infrastructure to accommodate growth.
   - Balancing quality with increased demand.
   - Managing the logistics of expansion.

3. Market Risks
   - Entering new markets with unknown variables.
   - Dealing with shifts in market dynamics.
   - Facing increased competition.

4. Team Management
   - Hiring and training new employees.
   - Ensuring team alignment with your brand values.
   - Delegating responsibilities effectively.

5. Maintaining Quality
   - Preserving the quality and consistency of your offerings.
   - Meeting customer expectations during growth.
   - Avoiding quality control issues.

Problem-Solving Strategies

When faced with these challenges, consider these strategies for effective navigation:

6. Financial Planning
   - Develop a robust financial plan for expansion.
   - Explore funding options such as loans, investors, or grants.
   - Maintain a financial cushion for unforeseen challenges.

7. Scalability Solutions
   - Continuously assess your scalability and adapt as needed.
   - Automate processes to handle increased demand efficiently.
   - Streamline your operations and workflows.

8. Market Research and Risk Management
   - Conduct in-depth market research and feasibility studies.
   - Develop contingency plans to address potential market risks.

   - Stay informed about industry trends and shifts.

9. Team Building
   - Carefully select and onboard new team members.
   - Train and communicate your brand values and expectations.
   - Foster a positive and collaborative team culture.

10. Quality Maintenance
   - Implement rigorous quality control measures.
   - Continuously monitor and assess the quality of your offerings.
   - Seek customer feedback and use it to make improvements.

Adapting to Challenges

Adaptability is crucial during expansion:

11. Flexibility
   Stay flexible in your approach and be open to adjusting your strategies in response to challenges and changing circumstances.

12. Problem-Solving Mindset
   Encourage a problem-solving mindset within your team, fostering the ability to tackle challenges head-on.

13. Learning from Setbacks
   Accept that setbacks and failures may occur. Use them as opportunities to learn and grow.

Seeking Support and Guidance

Don't hesitate to seek support and guidance when navigating challenges:

14. Mentorship

Connect with experienced mentors or advisors who can provide valuable insights and guidance.

15. Industry Networks

Join industry associations and networks to learn from peers who have faced similar challenges.

16. Peer Collaboration

Collaborate with other entrepreneurs and business owners who can share their experiences and solutions.

Conclusion

Expanding your side hustle into your main hustle is a significant step in your entrepreneurial journey. While it comes with challenges, it also offers the potential for growth, increased impact, and greater success.

In the chapters that follow, we'll explore how to manage and maintain your brand's values, quality, and consistency during expansion. By effectively navigating challenges and staying true to your vision, you'll be well-prepared to achieve your goals and make your passion profitable.

Remember that every challenge you face is an opportunity to learn, adapt, and ultimately strengthen your business. Approach each obstacle with a problem-solving mindset, and you'll be on the path to success.

13

Navigating Challenges in Expansion

In Chapter 12 of "From Side Hustle to Main Hustle: Making Your Passion Profitable," we explore the common challenges that arise as you expand your side hustle and offer strategies for effectively navigating these obstacles.

Common Challenges:

1. Financial Challenges: This includes securing funding, managing increased operating costs, and dealing with cash flow issues during growth.
2. Scalability: Adapting processes and infrastructure to accommodate growth, maintaining quality, and managing logistics.
3. Market Risks: Challenges associated with entering new markets, coping with shifts in market dynamics, and facing increased competition.
4. Team Management: Hiring, training, and aligning a growing team with your brand values.
5. Maintaining Quality: Preserving the quality and consistency of your offerings, meeting customer expectations, and avoiding quality control issues.

Problem-Solving Strategies:

6. Financial Planning: Develop a robust financial plan, explore funding options, and maintain a financial cushion.

7. Scalability Solutions: Continuously assess scalability, automate processes, and streamline operations.

8. Market Research and Risk Management: Conduct in-depth market research, develop contingency plans, and stay informed about industry trends.

9. Team Building: Carefully select and onboard new team members, train them on brand values, and foster a positive team culture.

10. Quality Maintenance: Implement quality control measures, monitor and assess product quality, and use customer feedback for improvements.

Adapting to Challenges:

11. Stay flexible, maintain a problem-solving mindset, and embrace setbacks as opportunities for learning and growth.

Seeking Support and Guidance:

14. Consider mentorship from experienced individuals.

15. Join industry networks and associations to learn from peers.

16. Collaborate with other entrepreneurs to share experiences and solutions.

Remember that every challenge you encounter presents an opportunity for growth and learning. Embrace each obstacle with a problem-solving mindset, and you'll be well-prepared to navigate the challenges of expansion while staying true to your vision.

The chapter emphasizes the importance of adaptability, learning from setbacks, and seeking support as you expand your side hustle into your main hustle.